Pictorial Archive of
LACE
DESIGNS

325 Historic Examples

Selected and Arranged by

Carol Belanger Grafton

Dover Publications, Inc.
New York

Copyright © 1989 by Dover Publications, Inc.
All rights reserved under Pan American and International
Copyright Conventions.

Published in Canada by General Publishing Company, Ltd.,
30 Lesmill Road, Don Mills, Toronto, Ontario.
Published in the United Kingdom by Constable and Company, Ltd.

Pictorial Archive of Lace Designs: 325 Historic Examples
is a new work, first published by Dover Publications, Inc., in 1989.

DOVER *Pictorial Archive* SERIES

This book belongs to the Dover Pictorial Archive Series. You
may use the designs and illustrations for graphics and crafts applications,
free and without special permission, provided that you include no more
than ten in the same publication or project. (For permission for
additional use, please write to Dover Publications, Inc., 31 East 2nd
Street, Mineola, N.Y. 11501.)
However, republication or reproduction of any illustration by any
other graphic service, whether it be in a book or in any other design
resource, is strictly prohibited.

Manufactured in the United States of America
Dover Publications, Inc., 31 East 2nd Street,
Mineola, N.Y. 11501

Library of Congress Cataloging-in-Publication Data

Pictorial archive of lace designs :
325 historic examples / selected and arranged by Carol Belanger Grafton.
p.   cm. — (Dover pictorial archive series)
ISBN 0-486-26112-3
1. Lace and lace making—Patterns.   I. Grafton, Carol Belanger.
II. Series.
TT800.P53   1989   89-16860
746.2'2—dc20   CIP

PUBLISHER'S NOTE

THE EARLY HISTORY OF LACE must be traced primarily through references in literature and household accounts and through representations in art, since, due to the fragility of lace, few early examples remain. When you add to this the fact that early accounts make little distinction between lace and other forms of needlework, it is easy to understand why the origins of lace cannot be pinpointed with any accuracy.

Although examples of netting have been found in Egyptian tombs, lacemaking is basically a European art. Certain types of openwork—drawnwork, darned netting, macramé and cutwork, for example—were well known in Europe late in the middle ages; however, lace, as we understand the term today, appears to have first been made and worn in the sixteenth century.

Just exactly what constitutes lace is a matter of some controversy. Certainly, the common definition of lace as an ornamental, openwork fabric made of fine thread is open to a great deal of interpretation. Although in popular parlance this definition is fairly loosely applied, according to purists there are only two major types of "real" lace— needlepoint lace and bobbin lace. In needlepoint lace, a single thread is used to work the design. The pattern is drawn on parchment or paper, then outlined with a heavy thread. This thread is then covered with buttonhole stitches. In contrast, several threads are used to make bobbin lace. The threads are wound onto bobbins and attached to a pillow or cushion, then twisted together following a pricked pattern fastened to the pillow.

Most experts will agree that lacemaking reached its highest level in the seventeenth century. Italy, particularly Venice, was the major producer of needlepoint lace, and the elaborate Venetian laces became the standard of perfection.

Although the emphasis was on needlepoint lace, the bobbin lace industry, based primarily in Flanders, also flourished during the seventeenth century, as those who could not afford needlepoint lace turned to the less expensive bobbin laces.

As the lacemaking industry spread throughout Europe, the new factories attempted to copy the Venetian patterns exactly. Soon, however, each factory developed its own individual characteristics, and new varieties of lace appeared. The French factories, particularly, became noted for the beauty and fineness of their product, and French laces began to rival Venetian laces.

The lacemaking industry developed in fits and starts for a number of reasons. As a luxury item, lace fell under the jurisdiction of the many sumptuary laws passed through-out Europe at various times. Although few of these laws, whose purpose was to discourage extravagance, lasted for long, their effect on the lacemaking industry was always disastrous. Political upheaval, too, played a part, particularly in France, where religious persecution of Protestants in the late seventeenth century drove many people, including many lacemakers, from the country. And, of course, the vagaries of fashion have always influenced the demand for lace.

The introduction of machine-made net in the early years of the nineteenth century changed the lacemaking industry completely. New types of lace developed, as handmade lace motifs were appliquéd to machine-made net, and, as technology became more sophisticated, lace produced entirely by machine appeared. As these inexpensive varieties of lace became widely available, the demand for handmade lace declined. Attempts to compete with the lower-priced machine-made laces, led to a deterioration in the materials and designs used for handmade lace. Although large amounts of handmade lace were produced up until World War I, it never again enjoyed the position it held in the seventeenth and eighteenth centuries.

Certain types of lace have also been produced in the home as well as commercially. Although needlepoint lace has rarely been worked by amateurs, the simpler forms of bobbin lacemaking have long been popular with needleworkers. In addition, in the late nineteenth and early twentieth century, the making of "modern" laces, which attempted to imitate the needlepoint laces of an earlier age, became a craze. These laces, the best known of which is Battenberg lace, were made by basting a machine-made tape to a paper pattern and filling in the resulting spaces with lace stitches. Although looked down on by lace experts, such laces were very popular and could be extremely beautiful when well done.

Today, there is a renewed interest in lace and lacemaking. Old lace is a sought-after collector's item, and lacemaking is once more a popular pastime. This book contains over 300 beautiful examples of lace, drawn from sources ranging from a sixteenth-century pattern book to nineteenth- and early twentieth-century women's magazines. Photographs of actual samples and sketches of designs for lace illustrate a wide variety of types, and bobbin lace, needlepoint lace, machine-made lace, net darning and "modern" lace are all represented. The designs include the geometric forms of the early laces, the heavy elaborate motifs of the seventeenth century, the graceful, fluid designs of the Art Nouveau period and all the styles between. It is our hope that this book will be a source of readily usable illustrations for graphic designers, a source of inspiration to lacemakers and a source of pleasure for those who love the beauty of this delicate art form.

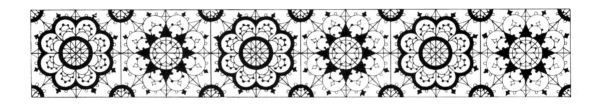

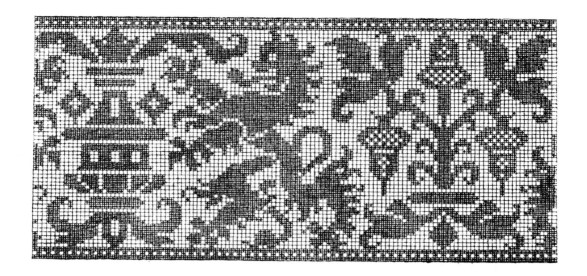

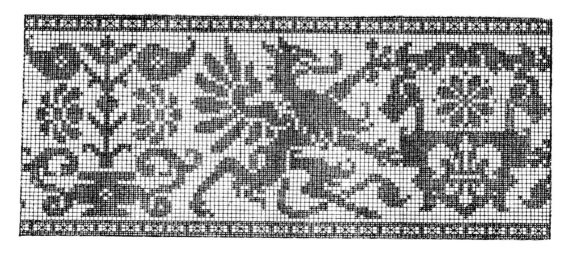

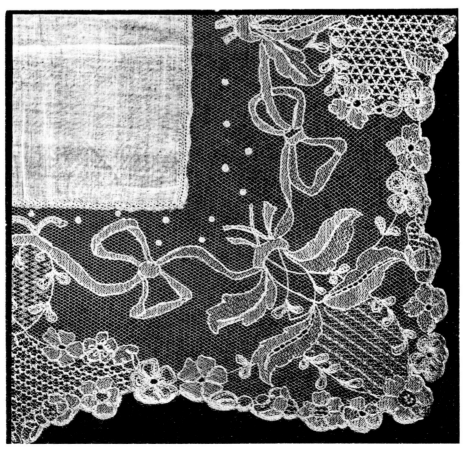

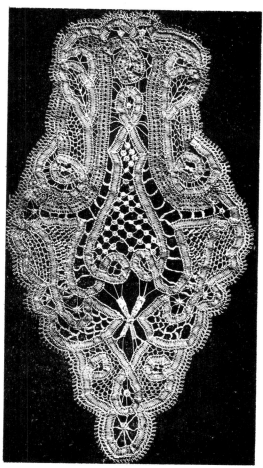

15

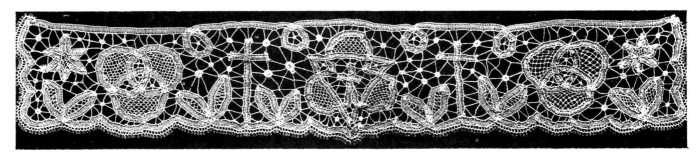

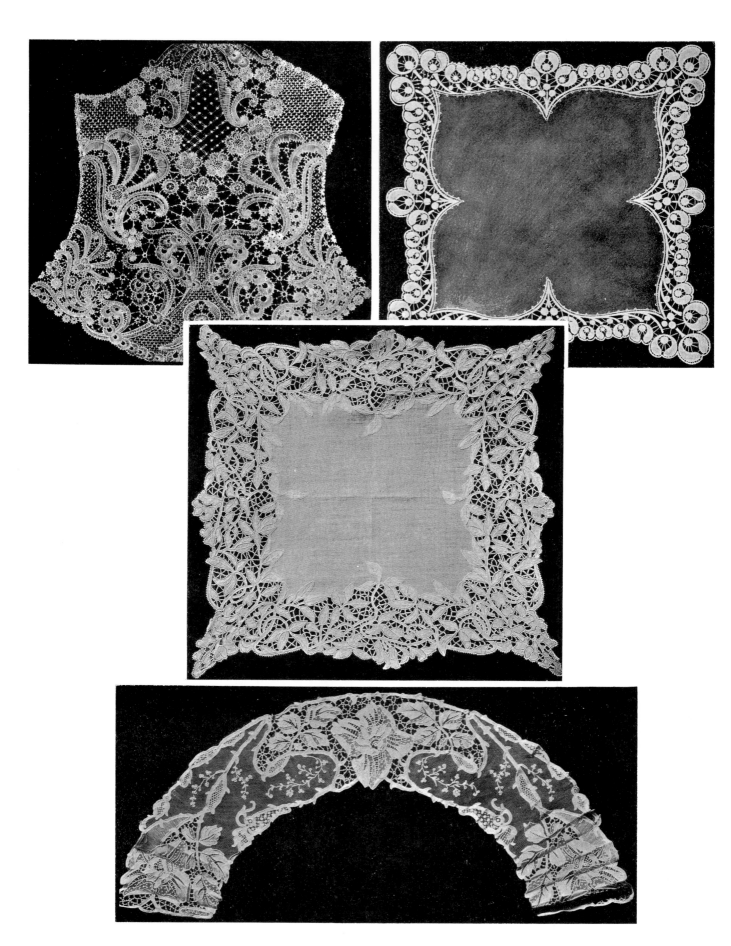

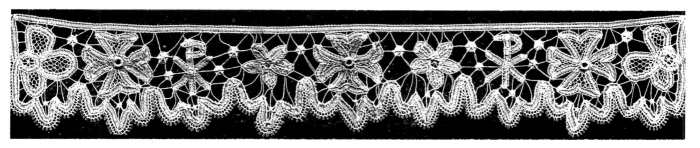

23

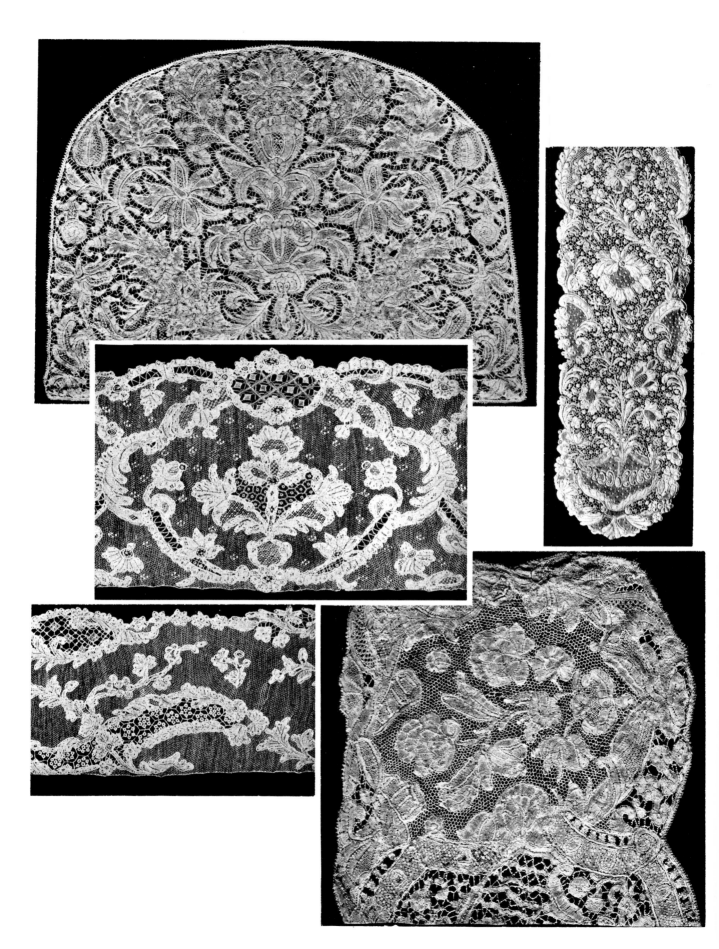

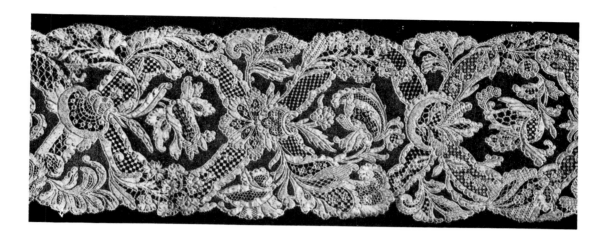

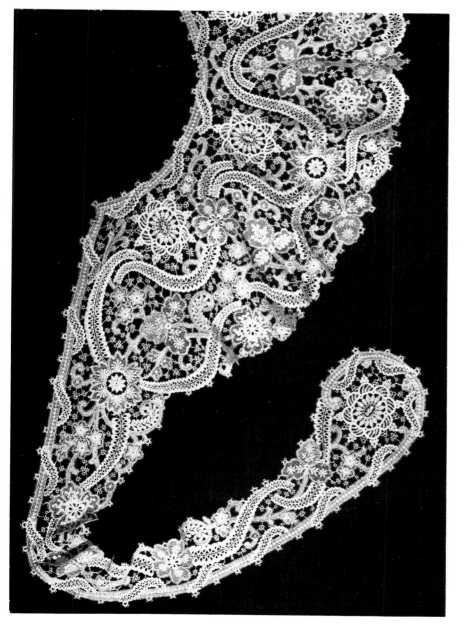

30

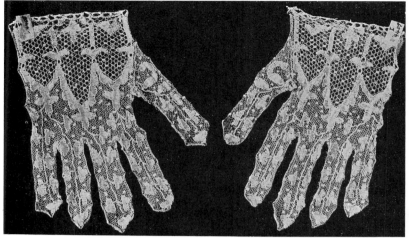

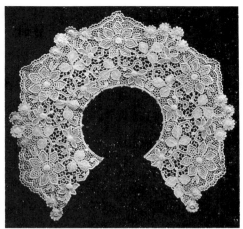

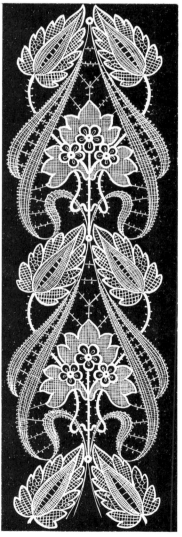

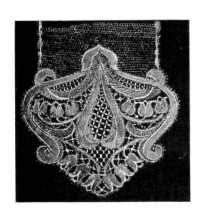

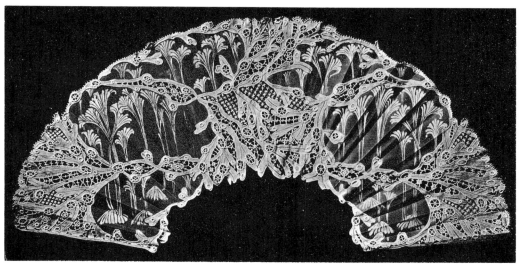

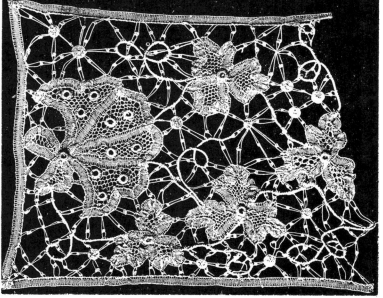

39

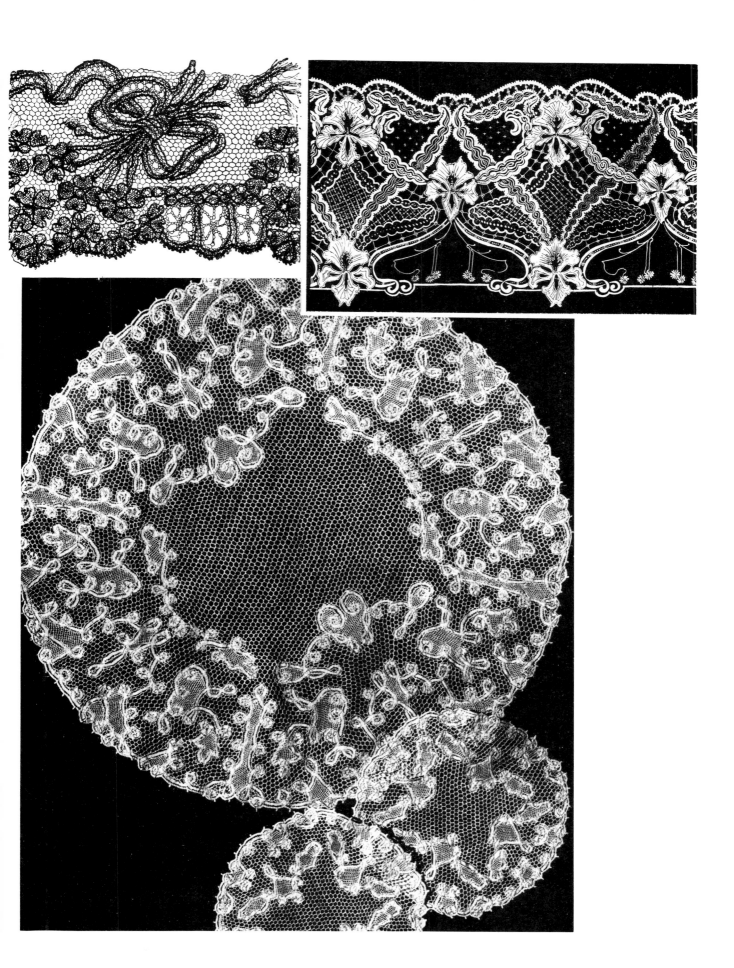

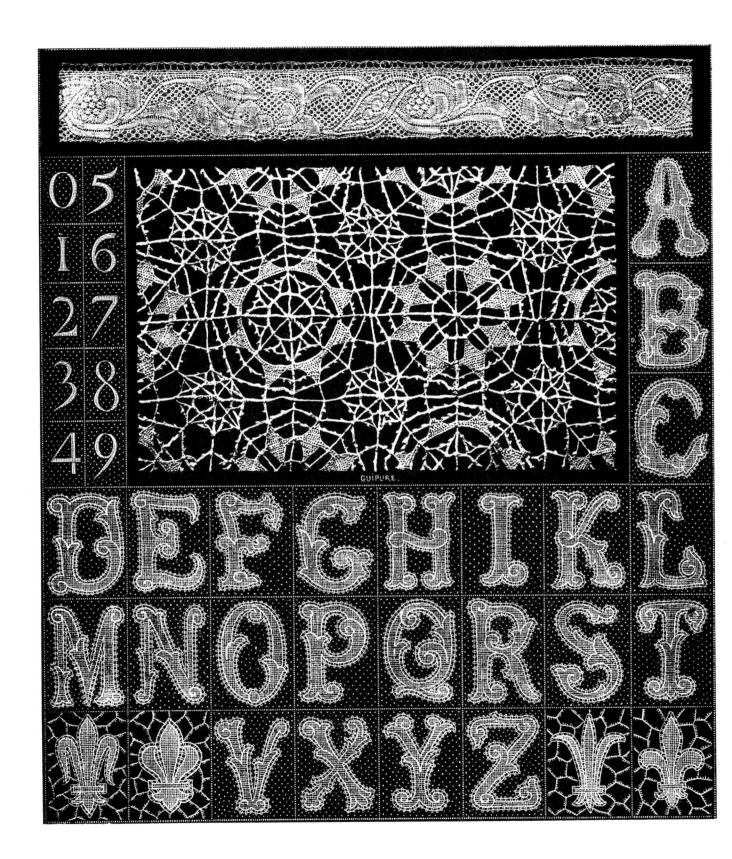

GUIPURE.

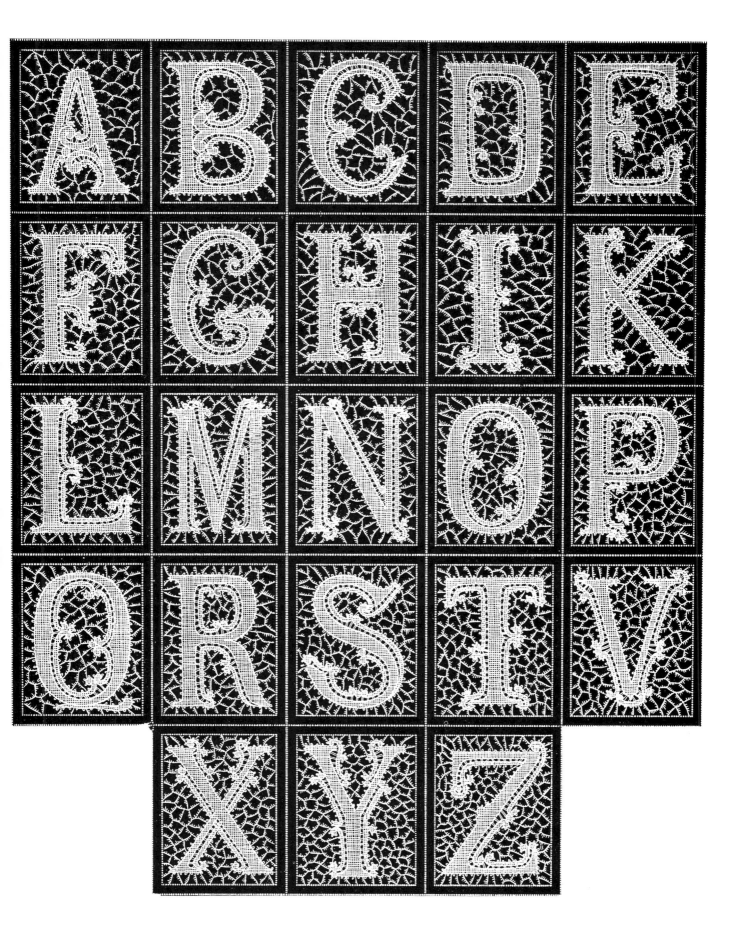

47

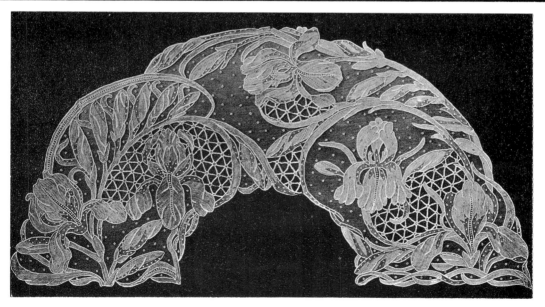

51

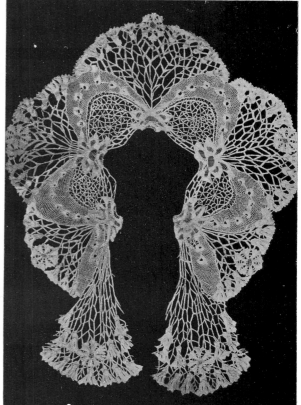

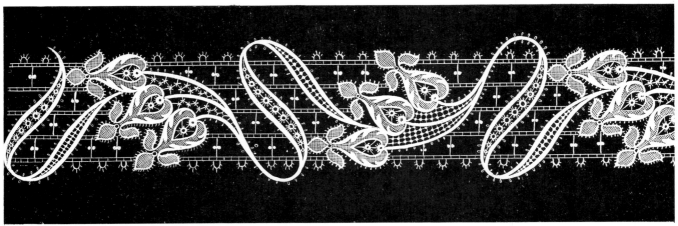

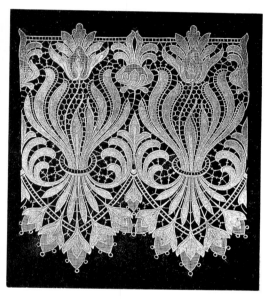

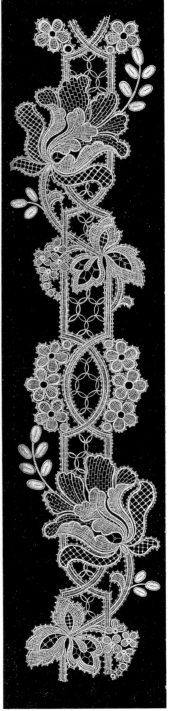

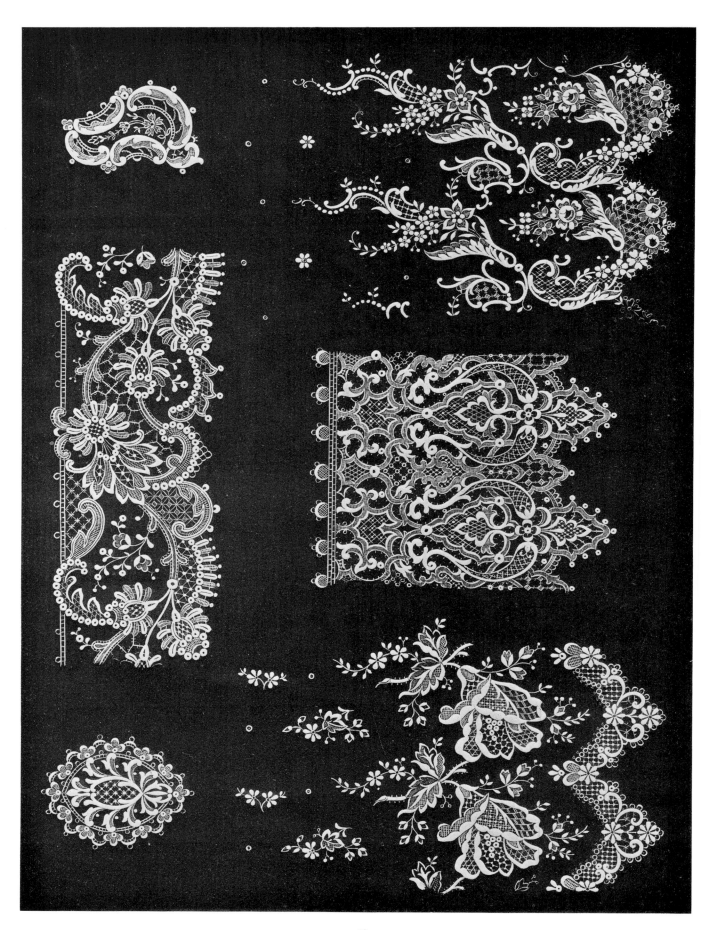

63

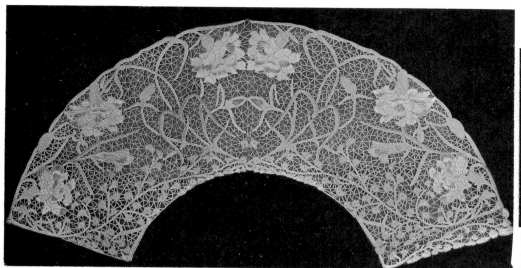

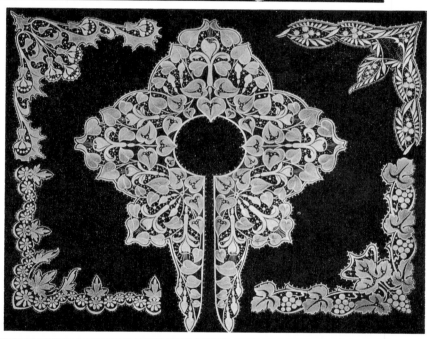

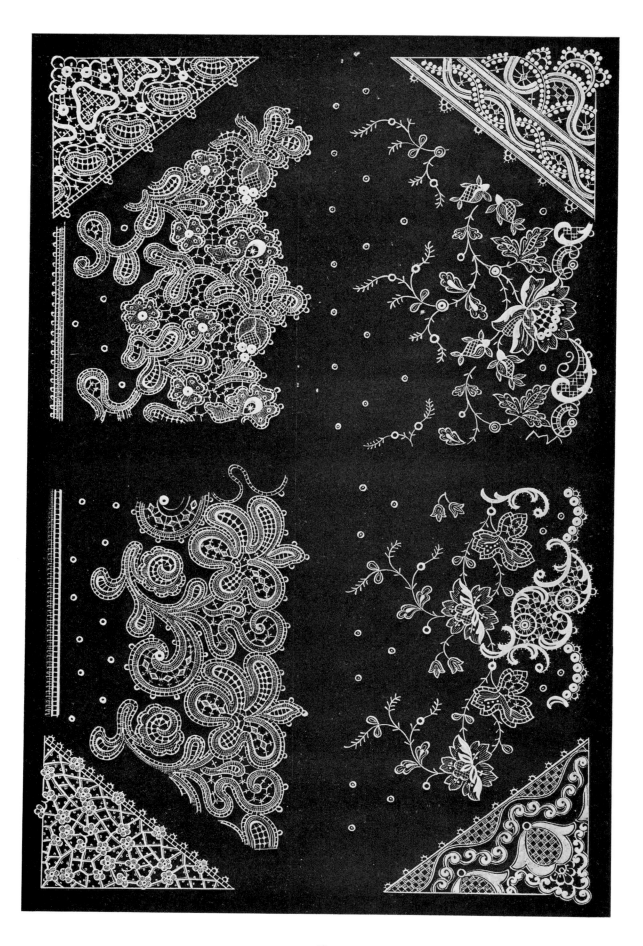

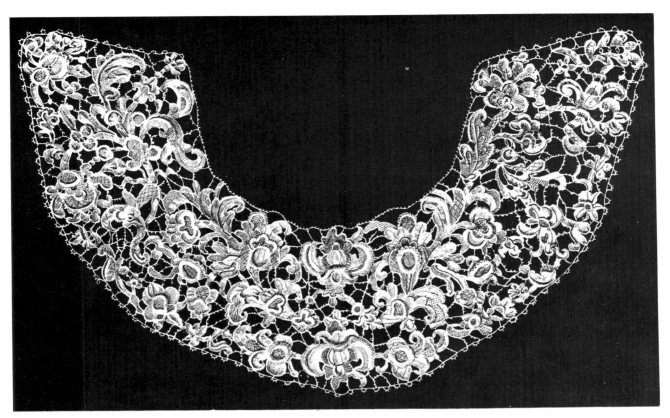

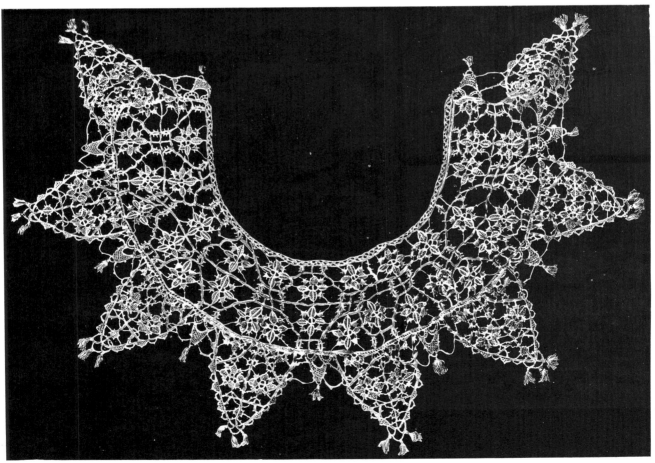

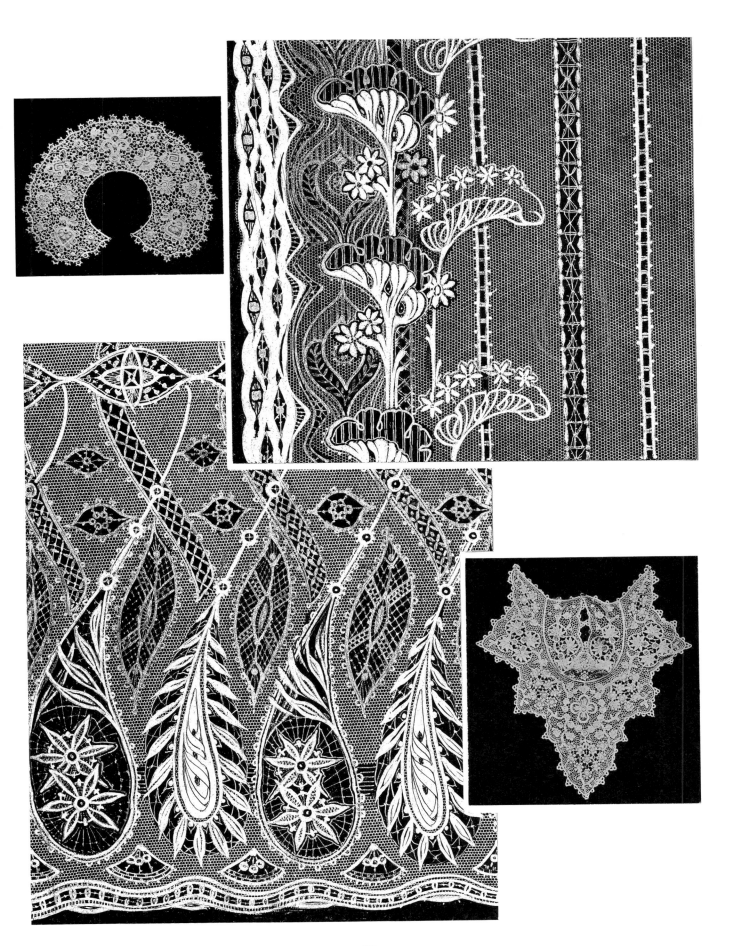

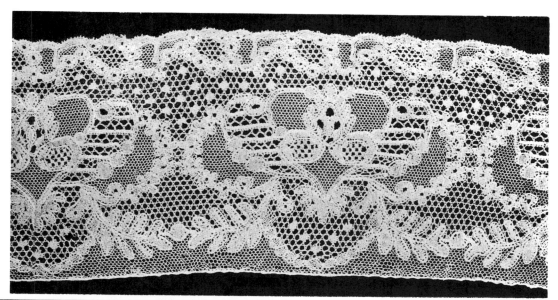

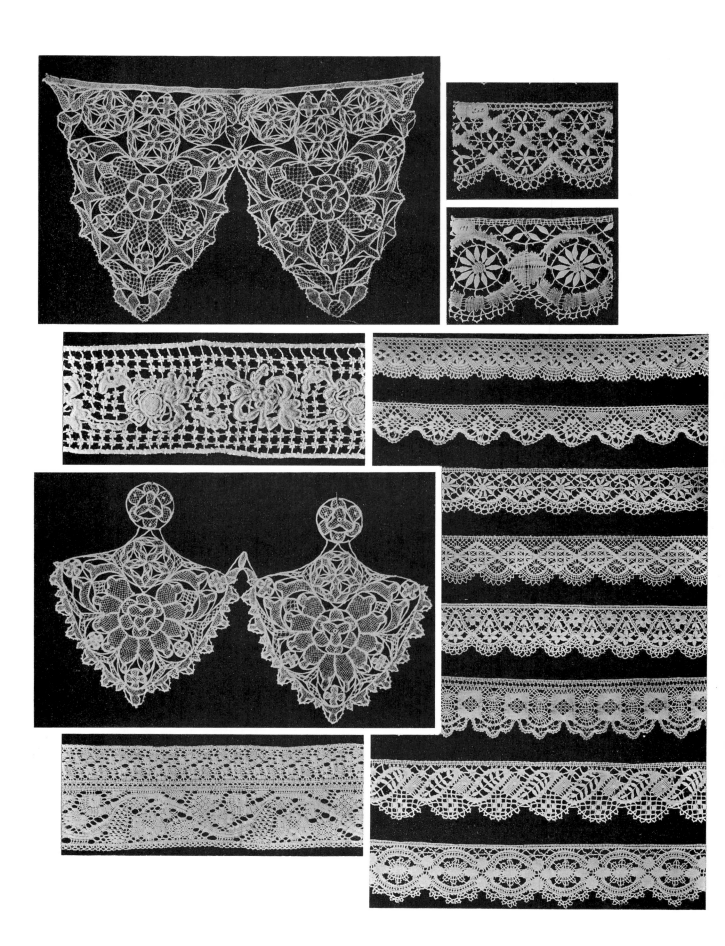

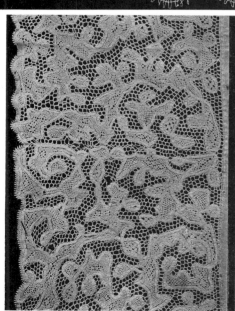